URBAN TALES OF THE BIBLE SHORT STORY SERIES BOOK 3 - THE SEX CRAVED HOMOCIDAL KING

MAY 8, 2022
Written by T.S. HOLDER

Copyright @ 2022 by T.S. Holder

All rights reserved. Written permission must be secured from the publisher to use or reproduce any part of this book.

The Bible stories and version used in this publication were accessed, respectively, through https://www.biblegateway.com and "Scripture taken from *The Message*. Copyright © 1993, 1994, 1995, 1996, 2000, 2001, 2002. Used by permission of NavPress Publishing Group."

Printed in the United States of America

ISBN 9798-9854404-5-4

This book series is dedicated to all of the elders in my family line. Those that have gone before us and those that are still here. Thank you for leaving a strong and powerful legacy of loving Yeshua.

If you would like TS Holder to do a live reading and/or for autographed copies email TS Holder at Suprnatrl@gmail.com and put TS Holder - Live Reading or TS Holder - Autographed Copies in the subject line.

Introduction

This story may seem a little familiar to those of you who are aware of what might be going on behind closed doors. Today it takes a person of high moral standards, usually a whistleblower, to leak stories of corruption to the press or other media outlets that will make them known to the public.

Often times the stories are leaked years after it actually happened and when it hits the media and the news outlets it is often labeled as a scandal, and most of the public will have an ah-ha moment making statements like, "I knew it was something funny about that. It just didn't seem right. I knew something wasn't clean in that milk!"

Well, in book three, of the short story series, quite a bit went on behind closed doors in the Royal Palace! I am pretty sure that the servants were aware of the goings on and you can bet that they talked among themselves on a regular! We all know how the saying that goes telegram, telephone tell somebody else and the story is gone. YASS news of this kind travels fast! The "Real Deal" is what was done to cover the shady mess up!! True Crime!!

This sounds like something that we need to step right into! This time I think that I will go out on the patio with a cool glass of strawberry lemonade and a bowl of chips n mango dip. It's time to flip the pages!

2 Samuel 11 & 12 – The Sex Craved Homicidal King

Well, it was that time of year once again when King David's men had to go out into the United Streets of Rabbah and bring the heat and smoke to the Ammonites. You see the Ammonites was one of the nations, along with the Moabites, that came as a result of the incestuous sexual relationship that Lot, Abraham's nephew, and his just too nasty daughters had when they were up in the mountains after Sodom and Gomorrah was destroyed and burned to the ground. This story was in part one of the original Urban Tales series.

The oldest daughter's son was named Moab, which means from father, and the youngest daughter's son was named Ben-Ammi, which means son of my people. Ben-Ammi was also known as Ammon, thus we have the Ammonites.

The Ammonites carried on the ways of Sodom and Gomorrah (wickedness) and their gods were Milcom (1 & 2 Kings) and Molech (2 Kings, Leviticus, Jeremiah, and Acts). Molech was considered a fire-god and the statute's face was half calf and half human. Also, the statute of Molech was in a sitting position with outstretched arms. Molech's arms were molded that way so that the babies, children and adults that were to be sacrificed to him could be placed in those arms and burned alive. It is said that the most sacrificed humans were babies. That right there is some crazy stuff!

But this begs the question what were the ways of Sodom and Gomorrah? According to

Ezekiel 16:49 the ways of Sodom and Gomorrah was being prideful, arrogant, eating too much food, being lazy and not helping the poor and others that were in need of help. Jude 1:7 says that Sodom and Gomorrah and the towns surrounding them engaged in sexual perversion and wickedness. Jeremiah 23:14 compares the prophets of Jerusalem to Sodom and Gomorrah saying that they commit adultery, were big time liars and of course they did nothing to help the poor but rather they put their resources towards helping those that were evil and performed evil works. There are many scriptures that describe the ways of Sodom and Gomorrah, but the one thing that all the scriptures have in common is that the ways of Sodom and Gomorrah was evil and they had too much going on that was not honoring God.

With all of what was just described in the previous paragraph we can see that the Ammonites had a lot going on. They were doing the most when it came to being outright evil. There was no way that the Ammonites could just cold turkey stop all that craziness, how could they, they didn't even acknowledge the God of Israel.

Every year about the same time the Ammonites just had to pull up on their enemies, the Israelites and any allies of the Israelites to try and bring smoke. The Ammonites were pushing to takeover and rule everyone, everywhere. They wanted everyone to bow to them and partake in their evil deeds either voluntarily or by force. Maybe it was their DNA and genes that had them in this constant state of craziness. Maybe because their beginning came from a man who was father and grandfather and from a woman who was mother and sister. That in itself is a lot to process and maybe, just maybe that was too much for their brains to handle and if you add in the ways and teachings of Sodom and Gomorrah then there is one big hot pot of ordure (poop) just boiling around in their brains and spirits.

Well, it was that time of year and King David sent his men to the capital city of the Ammonites, Rabbath or Rabbah, to kick some Ammonite badonkadonk. King David didn't ride out with them this time, he decided that he would stay back in Jerusalem and take care of military matters from there. He would receive daily messages from couriers who would carry information to him from the lines of war. David would have constant updates and with those updates he could make any strategic adjustments needed, such as sending out more souljahs.

I believe that David's big mistake was not riding out with his men to battle. Even though he was getting updates and making adjustments as needed, he was somewhat idle and we all know what is said about an idle mind. Well, we shall see if that statement holds true in this case.

David stayed behind and one particular day, a little late in the afternoon, David was feeling kind of tired and exhausted from managing the war and the kingdom, so he took a little mid-day nap and when he woke up he was feeling somewhat revived and rejuvenated. David stretched, yawned and said,

"Mmm...Nothing like a good old power nap to strengthen the body! Now I just need a little coffee or vanilla cappuccino to get me going."

David sent for his servant and said, "Hey, would you please bring me a cup of coffee or better yet make that a cup of vanilla cappuccino and while you're at it make me some cinnamon toast and well done turkey sausage patties, please, to go along with it."

The servant left to go to the kitchen and David finally got outta the big puffy recliner, cleaned himself up and put some eye drops in to relieve his dry, tired, red eyes. He also decided to put on a little smell good, which always seems to make things better. Then David decided that he would take his Royal Hiney up to the Royal Palace roof top to walk around, look over his kingdom and get a bit of fresh air. It was a gorgeous day, a little crisp breeze was flowing and the crickets had their choir in full motion. David thought, "Man those crickets have it going on. Listen to the harmony and they even know exactly when to come in. They haven't missed a beat yet!

David had a beautiful view of Jerusalem from the Royal Palace roof top and he could see just about everything and everyone. Maybe he saw just a little too much!

Shortly after David started looking over his kingdom, the servant came back with David's order, put it down and began to walk away, but as he was leaving David stopped him dead in his tracks. David saw this beautiful sista with glistening golden tan skin, long twisted locks with a hint of amber streaks, and a slammin' body. David's mind and body woke all the way up! He quickly and immediately called his servant over to where he was standing and said, "Thanks for bringing my vanilla cappuccino, cinnamon toast and turkey sausage patties. They are just like I like them! But, hey, would you please take a look over there? You see right down there in that building next to the Town Café'! Do you see that stunningly gorgeous woman standing in the window looking out and gazing? Who is she? I really, really need to know who that angel of a sista is!"

The servant said, "Oh yeah. That's Bathsheba. She's the daughter of Eliam and Sir, she is a very happily married woman. She loves her husband."

David said, "Married! To whom? I mean who is this blessed and lucky man?"

The servant said, "Her husband is Uriah, the Hittite and as I said they are deeply in love. They have been together since middle school. Their story was actually featured in the Jerusalem News Society section. The story goes that they promised each other that they would always be together and that is exactly what they did. It must be extremely hard for her since Uriah was sent to war to fight the Ammonites because they have never been a part from each other."

David said, "Well, I am sure that it is hard on her, ya know, Uriah being at war with the rest of the troops. This being the first time that they have been apart it must be extra hard for her to be alone. Please go over there and bring Bathsheba to me at once. I would like to offer her words of comfort and assurance that Uriah will be alright, the war will be over soon and he will be home in her arms once again."

Now you see, David knew exactly what he was doing and had every opportunity to back away, but NAW he is the king and the king can do anything. The servant had already told David that the woman was married, but David knew that he had other motives, talkin' about offer her words of comfort and encouragement. REALLY! He knew that he should not have sent for her. He should have kept looking around his kingdom or even go get one of his many side chick concubines from the Concubine quarters, but NAW he just had to get with Bathsheba, the married woman. He was king so he felt that he could do what he wanted to do.

When the servant left the palace roof, he went directly to the kitchen where the other servants were and said, "King David is at it again! DUDE is just too much! This time he has his eyes on poor innocent Bathsheba. I don't know why he does this type of thing, maybe it's just because he is king and he can or he has a terrible lustful sex demon?"

One of the female servants said, "Ya know it is truly ashamed. He gets these women, sleeps with them and then they become just another side chick that lives in the Concubine quarters and the poor people of the kingdom pay high taxes for them to be at his disposal! Now he has his eyes on Bathsheba? You did tell him that she is happily married?"

The male servant said, "Bruh, I told him the entire story, even how Bathsheba and Uriah were featured in Jerusalem News Society section and have been together since Middle School. That didn't seem to matter to him. You know how he is, he wants what he wants and he gets what he wants! He is so taken by her beauty that he just has to have her. He wants me to go and bring her to him. The things that we are asked to do around this place! When I hit the lottery King Freaky and nem can forget my name and face! "

The rest of the servants shook their heads and started sending up silent prayers for Bathsheba. They had all seen the secret room where David took the ladies when he first got with them and all of the whips and chains and other sex objects that he had in that room. That's why the servants often referred to him as King Freaky.

Once Bathsheba was brought to David, he didn't waste any time gettin' with this married beauty. David said, "Good afternoon. How are you doing this FINE day?"

Bathsheba answered, "I am doing good sir. I miss my husband who is at war in Rabbath against those worrisome inbred Ammonites."

David said, "I can SEE that you are doing just FINE and I am sorry to hear that you miss your husband. Uriah is performing a duty that every man has to this kingdom and that is to protect it against our enemies."

Bathsheba agreed and said, "Yes, you are right, but it does not make the pain of loneliness any better."

David responded as he slouched down in the couch, "Please excuse my manners, I am so taken by your beauty that I forgot to ask if I could get you anything?"

Bathsheba replied, "No thank you, sir, I am good. I ate a late lunch and had a glass of wine with it."

David replied, "Ok. If you are sure, but if you change your mind please let me know. We have the best of everything here. You know, Bathsheba, earlier today I was standing on my rooftop looking out over the kingdom and I noticed you standing in your window looking out. I noticed how beautiful you are, but your beauty was marred by the overwhelming sad look that you have in your eyes."

At that moment Bathsheba pulled her scarf around her face in an attempt to hide her eyes.

David said, "Yes, that look right there. So that is one of the reasons I had my servant to bring you to me. I wanted to bring you here to assure you that your husband Uriah will be fine and will be home in your arms soon enough. The war shouldn't take too long to win and he will be home with his fine bae in his arms. My servant told me all about your story of love and how this is the first time that you two have been apart. This has to be very hard for the both of you!"

Bathsheba answered, "Yes. This is truly very hard. I miss him so very much. We have never been apart and the nights are the worse. I miss his touch, his warmth and his smell. I just love him so much. I pray so hard for him every day and many times throughout the day. I need him to come home to me in one piece and healthy physically and mentally."

Bathsheba started to tear up and her face turned red from holding it back. She whimpered just a bit but then was able to reel her feelings back in.

David responded, "Oh my dear beautiful baby, I mean lady, don't cry. But if you must cry come a little closer that I may offer you comfort and encouragement. You don't have to stand all the way over there. I am your king and I will not harm you, so come a little closer and sit here next to me."

Bathsheba was very reluctant to get any closer to David because she and the entire Kingdom had heard about King David's "Sex-capades." The "SECRET" room that David had all of his sex equipment in was not as much a secret as he thought it was. The servants had taken it upon themselves to give intimate details of the equipment and what it was used for. They even gave specific examples, but they were discrete enough to leave out the names of the many ladies that David had ruined.

One of the servants had a detailed journal that gave accounts by date and with names. This lady servant left nothing out. She said that the journal was for her retirement and planned to publish it once she left the service of the king. Every now and then she would have a Journal party and would read a few pages, but she wouldn't tell it all because she didn't want anyone else taking her idea and running with it. The other servants often wondered how she knew so many details. What the other servants didn't know is that this particular servant found one of the hidden passages in the Royal Palace that led to a room that was directly adjacent to the sex room. She would go there 2-3 times per week, watch, listen and write down every single detail. When I say every detail, she wrote every detail. Gurlfriend had every intention of telling it all and getting rich in the process. I certainly hoped the participants enjoyed themselves because when the news comes out, it will be on and poppin' and they can ask themselves if it was really worth it. Smart lady!! I hope that she uses a pen name like TS Holder did!!

Here again David knew that this woman was married. He could see how much she missed her man even to the point of tears. David had many other women that he could have entertained himself with, but NAW he had to ruin a happy marriage and taken advantage of a grieving wife. The woman was happily married and did not want to be forced into the act of betraying her honey, Uriah, who was at war. She moved slowly and reluctantly towards David who was all slouched down on the couch. Eventually, with David coaxing her, she sat next to

David, after all he was the King and she couldn't refuse him.

David said, "Now see isn't that better. You can take a load off of your feet while we talk and I wipe your tears. So tell me more of your life with Uriah."

Bathsheba said, "Well, King, we have known each other since grade school. We actually made a vow to stay together while we were in middle School and we have kept our vow. We have been true to each other and are deeply in love with each other. We are the exclamation marks to each other's existence. Life without him would not be life, but rather it would be existing without a purpose."

David said, "Wow. That is amazing! The king needs someone like you in his life. Being in charge can be oh so lonely."

Bathsheba said, "Well, what about all of the side chicks that you have living in Concubine quarters, that the citizens of the kingdom pay high taxes to have live here, what about them? Why do you have them if you are still lonely?"

David replied, "Well, young innocent lady, the concubines are for other things. The king needs someone that will have his back and be with him on those lonely nights. I need someone that I can talk to, someone that gets me the way that you get Uriah. I need something real for a change and I believe that you are the real change."

Bathsheba replied, "No sir, I am not. Uriah has my heart and I am his exclamation point and only his. I pray that God brings that special someone into your life, but until you stop with your sex-capades you probably won't find her."

David said, "What do you know about that? You can't talk to me in that manner!"

Bathsheba said, "The entire kingdom knows what you do up in here. And yes, you crossed the line by comin' for me and pushin' up on me, so yes I can talk to you that way."

David was now livid and besides himself. At that moment David let his hands do the talking and as unwilling as Bathsheba was she knew that David was king and also her body was responding to

David's touches. Before she knew it she and David were in his bed in a mad moment of passion which lead to David taking her to the secret room. This moment occurred seven days after Bathsheba's monthly so she was considered to be pure.

When it was all said and done Bathsheba felt embarrassed and royally betrayed! Her heart was hurting because she knew that she had betrayed her husband Uriah! David on the other hand was pleased with himself, smiling and living in the moment of what had just happened and because he had gotten what he wanted, but David did not consider if God was pleased with him?

Bathsheba cleaned herself up, got dressed, looked at David lying there with a glass of wine in his hand looking pleased with himself and she left.

She cried all the way home. She was embarrassed because she knew that not only did the servants know what had happened, but so did those who saw her walking home. David didn't even have the decency to send her home in a Royal Uber!

The servants were talking again. The head servant said, "He should be ashamed of himself. Poor Bathsheba left here crying and clutching her wedding ring."

The Journalist servant said, "The things that he did to her were just not right. God will take care of David, because only God can get with a king."

David carried on his regular routine like nothing ever happened, but what happened between he and Bathsheba was tearing Bathsheba apart. She never wanted to step outside of her marriage and to make matters worse some weeks later she found out that she was pregnant.

Bathsheba sent word that she needed to see the king. David granted her request to see him because in his mind he thought that she was coming back for more. Really David, really!! Bathsheba went to the palace and David said, "Good afternoon! How can I help you? Do you need anything? I have been sending you extra food, perfumes and gifts to let you know that I enjoyed our time together and want to continue what we have going on. Is that why you are here? If so it is too early in the day and I have many things concerning war to complete, but after that I am all yours. You are welcome to stay here until I am done!"

Bathsheba replied, "I never responded to your gifts because I feel that I betrayed my husband and you betrayed me. Uriah is out there fighting for both of us and this is what we did to him! It just wasn't right and on top of that you impregnated me! I am pregnant. This is your child because I have not been with anyone else but my husband and when he finds out he might kill me and come for you. Uriah don't play that messing around stuff."

David said, "Not so loud. The staff may over hear you. Ear hustlin' is still a gainful hustle. You are pregnant? Well, I don't have a problem with that. The child will be beautiful. Look at the mother, not to mention the father! No need to worry I will take care of everything. Don't worry about your husband. I am the king. I got this, I got you! I got us!"

David thought about how he would go about resolving this issue and of course being the chess player that he is, he came up with a plan. Once the daily courier arrived with word from the front lines David sent a message back to his nephew and military leader Joab, that same day. In this message David said, "Joab I need you to send Uriah the Hittite back to Jerusalem. There are matters here that I need to discuss with him."

When Joab received the message the same day, he thought that it was very unusual because couriers take messages of what is happening in the war to the king but none is received back until the next day and what on earth could he possibly have to discuss with Uriah? BUT his uncle was the king and he had to obey him, so he sent Uriah back to Jerusalem that same day.

When Uriah found out that he was going back home, he was not at all happy to leave his fellow soldiers there fighting while he was to go home and enjoy the comforts of home. He was happy that he would see his beautiful wife, but he didn't want to leave the ongoing war. Uriah felt that he was shirking his duties by going back home.

Uriah came to King David and said, "Sir, I am here."

David said, "Great to see that you are all in one piece and you haven't been hurt or anything. So tell me what is going on in this war? Have the strategies that I am sending Joab working?"

Uriah said, "As far as I can tell we are bringing the smoke and the Ammonites don't stand a chance."

David said, "Great. I hear that you are one of the top soldiers out there and I wanted to award you for being the top soldier."

Uriah said, "Me? The top soldier? There are many others that do far more and that have better warrior skills than I do. How did you pick me? I am in the back of the war, washing dishes and cooking, what is so top soldier-ish about that?"

David said, "It is just as important that the soldiers get a good meal to fuel their bodies and that the dishes are clean so that no one gets sick while they are out there. You are the best that you can be in what you do! So today, since you are here, go on home, get cleaned up, and I will have a special meal and wine sent to you and your wife. Then afterwards spend some quality time with your wife. You two are so in love and have never been apart, so enjoy this moment with her. That is a Royal Order!"

You see Uriah was an honorable man at heart, he heard exactly what the king said but he couldn't bring himself to go home. Uriah just wasn't feeling this! Now, don't get it twisted, he loved his wife and thought of her often while he was in the war, but he felt as though he was betraying his buddies that were out there sleeping on the ground and fighting the Ammonites, so in his heart he knew that there was no way that he could go home and sleep in his comfy bed and make love to his gorgeous wife. He couldn't bring himself to do it, so Uriah slept right outside of the palace! He found himself an empty room in servant's quarters and camped out there. He did not go home! Uriah thought to himself, "This is awfully nice of the king, but who am I to receive such privileges during war time? Why did he choose me? I mean, I appreciate the honor and all, but there are men out there who are far greater cooks and warriors than myself. Something just doesn't feel right about this."

Uriah tossed and turned all night long wondering what was going on in the battle and why was he taken out of the battle. He tossed so much that one of the other servants heard him and went into see who was in the spare room. The servant peeped around the corner and saw Uriah! Chile the servant went and woke up the others and they strolled on over to the Royal Kitchen to have a meeting.

The head servant said, "What is this about? It is one o'clock in the morning. This had better be important."

The servant that called the meeting said, "We were all just talking about Bathsheba and Uriah and what King Freakly did, well I heard some noise in the empty bedroom and lo and behold it is Uriah! Uriah is in there sleeping."

The servants gasped for air and said, "Man, stop playin'! It's too early in the morning for this now."

The servant bringing the news said, "For real, for real. I swear that it is him! What is he doing here?"

The head servant said, "OMG! It can only mean one thing!"

The female servants said, "This means that Bathsheba is pregnant and the king is trying his best to cover it up."

One of the other male servants said, "How did you get that? And what do you mean cover it up?"

The head female servant said, "We saw Bathsheba come back to the palace the other day and talk with David. Then we saw the courier come and go the same day instead of the next day. SO if Uriah is here, he is trying to get Uriah to sleep with Bathsheba so that it can appear to be Uriah's baby!"

The slow male servant said, 'No way! He wouldn't stoop that low, would he?"

They all looked at each other and said, "Oh yes he would and he did!"

The servants ended the meeting because they found that they only had a couple of hours before it was time to prepare breakfast. They all left the meeting shaking their heads and saying prayers for the young couple, Bathsheba and Uriah. They should have been praying for God to touch the heart and body of the king all along and maybe this wouldn't have happened.

The next morning one of the servants went to David and said, "Sir, Uriah slept all night long in one of the empty rooms in the servant's quarters. He tossed and turned and was even talking in his sleep. We couldn't quite make out what he was saying, but it was intense. Maybe he has PTSD from the battle. We knew that he was your guest so we thought that you might want to know."

David said, "Thank you so much for that information. Please get Uriah and bring him to me."

Uriah came into the palace where David was and said, "Good morning King David, you summoned me? Am I going back to battle now?"

David said, "Good morning Uriah. I heard that you had a very restless night and didn't go home to be with your wifey? I don't understand? I gave you the special honor of coming in from the war to spend some time with your wife and you sleep in an empty room with the servants? Please enlighten me."

Uriah said, "I just couldn't find it in my heart to go home and sleep in my comfortable bed and make love to my beautiful bae while my fellow soldiers are out there sleeping in tents and on the ground. I am a true soldier and there is no way that I could enjoy such pleasures while the others are out there suffering the pains of war! Why did you choose me for this? There are others that deserve it more than myself and so I understand there have only been a few others before me that have been honored in this way."

David said, "Wow! You are a true soldier with a heart of honor and integrity! I understand your concerns but I believe that you deserve this time with your wife and yes there have been a few others that I have honored this way."

David thought to himself, "How did he find out about the other men? Who told him and did they tell him the entire story?"

Uriah said, "But king, I really need to get back to war. This just doesn't feel right at all."

David replied, "But nothing! You will stay one more night and in the meantime let's eat and drink and enjoy life. Then I want you to go home to be with your wife!"

So David and Uriah ate and drank wine the majority of the day. Every time Uriah's glass fell empty David would have his servant fill it up. Uriah wasn't really a drinker so it wasn't long before he was sloppy drunk. David thought for sure that his plan had worked and now that Uriah was drunk he would go home to be with his wife.

I know by now that you all have figured out David's plan. He wanted Uriah to go home and sleep with Bathsheba so that it would look like Uriah got her pregnant and not him. This would have been a true war baby! One thing that I have noticed since writing this series is that there were some scheming, plotting, conniving, ear hustlin' folks in the Bible!

Uriah still wasn't having it. It is often said that a person's true feelings come out when they are drunk. Well, Uriah's feelings were the same as when he was sober. He did not want to go home and be with his wife. There was true honor in this man's heart. Uriah went back to the empty room to sleep, but found that someone else had taken it, so he grabbed one of the female servant's yoga mat and slept on the floor.

David had one of his servants to report Uriah's action to him. He wanted to be sure if Uriah went home or not. When the servant came back he said, "Sir, Uriah still didn't go home. We made sure that someone was in the empty room, but that didn't matter. Uriah took one of the yoga mats and slept on the floor. Sir, he is a true soldier at heart!"

David said, "I See! Thank you for the information, you are dismissed."

David thought to himself, "I didn't want to use plan B. All of the other men that I honored this way went on home and slept with their Bae's, but not this one do gooder! I hate to do it to him, but I gotta do what I gotta do."

So David sat down and prepared a letter to send back with the courier to his nephew Joab. David wrote in the letter, "Nephew and commander of my army, Uriah appears to be a fierce warrior. It is time that he is taken off of kitchen duty and placed into the fighting. I think that he would be better utilized if he was right out there in the front of the battle where things are the hottest! He appears to be able to handle himself and his weapons with great expertise so put him out there so that he can help in the place where the battle is the worst and where the Ammonites are doing the most damage! Once you have placed him there I want you and the other men to move on to another area where you are needed and let him handle it. He can do it. I really trust that with his skills he can handle it."

Uriah woke that morning with a hangover from hell! Since he wasn't a drinker he did not know what to do about that. One of the servants noticed how he was moving around and said, "Hey there! I see that you really got lit last night. I betcha gotta serious headache right about now?"

Uriah said, "Man my head is spinning and it aches, not to mention how weak my stomach is."

The servant mixed Uriah a little something to drink for that hangover and then gave him a nice meal to make him feel a little better. Just at that moment Uriah got word from the king that he was going back to battle. Uriah said, "Well, it's about time. I can finally go back to be with my fellow soldiers and fight. I got time to make up and Ammonites to kill. I am ready, headache, bad stomach and all! I am ready!"

When the courier arrived Joab had the Ammonites city of Rabbah under wraps. King

David's army was doing the most but the battle was still not over. Uriah rode back with the courier and reported to Joab.

Joab said, "It's great to see you back. Give me a moment please so that I can read this message from the King."

When Joab read the message he said to himself, "What is my uncle up to? Why is he telling me to put this young cook out there to fight the worst Ammonites and then leave him there to handle it! While Uriah has a warrior's heart his fighting skills leave a lot to be considered. The only thing that I have ever seen him use as a weapon is a frying pan and soap and water. I hate to do this, but I cannot disobey a direct order from the king."

Joab told Uriah, "I guess that the King was very impressed with you and feels that you are ready to go to the front lines and hold it down."

Uriah was so excited that he would finally get to do what he thought he came for. Uriah replied, "I am so glad that I didn't go home and sleep with my wife, if I had I would not have the strength to go out here and kick some Ammonite butt! Let's do this!"

Joab thought to himself, "Oh Lord, unc is at it again. I fully understand now. Uriah's wife must be pregnant by unc. My uncle the king has a weakness for pretty women and for unc to go to these lengths to cover it up, she must be one fine lady!"

So Uriah was sent to an area in the city of Rabbath where the Ammonites had the strongest hold. He fought like the fierce warrior that he thought in his mind and heart he was. He and the other men were making some head way and pushing the Ammonites back and just at that moment Joab and the others left Uriah there by himself!

Uriah was fighting hard and when he turned around looking for the others he found himself all alone. Uriah said to himself, "Was I fighting that hard that I didn't hear the command to leave the area? Why didn't one of my boys come and get me? They just left me here alone, now I am surrounded! Lord help me please! I should have gone to see my baby when King David ordered me to but I didn't know that, that would be my last opportunity to hold her and kiss her. Lord please let her know that I love her and that I died for her and my king."

The next morning Joab sent a message by the courier to David saying, "I have done what you asked and unfortunately Uriah was killed in battle. He fought fiercely but he was no match for the Ammonites!"

David sent a message back to Joab saying, "This is what happens in the heat of battle. Great warriors often die. I know that this is a great loss to you and your men but hold your head up and fight on. That is what Uriah would have wanted you all to do."

David then told his servant to bring Bathsheba to him because he wanted to be the first to tell her what had happened to Uriah. Once Bathsheba arrived David said, "Bathsheba, please come and sit with me."

Bathsheba sat down with David and David began to weave the story of how bravely Uriah fought to the death defending the kingdom, "Bathsheba my dear, I have brought you here to give you the news that I have received from the war. It seems that Uriah was promoted to the infantry from the kitchen and he was in one of the hottest areas of the war and somehow became detached from the company of men that he went in with. Once it was realized that he was not accounted for the team went back out to find him and found him. Uriah had been killed. He fought bravely in one of the hottest areas of the war and died defending you and the kingdom. He will receive a special honor for his bravery and you will also receive a monthly check for your loss. I wanted to be the one to tell you what happened, because I know how much you two loved each other."

Bathsheba began to cry and sob so loudly that she could be heard down in the kitchen area where the servants were. Once of the servants said, "What is that? Who is crying?"

The main servant said, "I brought Bathsheba into King David and at the request of the king I stood outside the door so that they wouldn't be disturbed. I overheard David tell Bathsheba that Uriah was killed in the war."

The female servant said, "Killed in the war or setup to be killed in the war? God is going to get David with a quickness for taking that man's life because of his sex-craved behavior! You just wait and see. Mock my word!"

Once Bathsheba had cried until there were no more tears she looked at David and said, "You did this didn't you? I remember you telling me 'No need to worry I will take care of everything. Don't worry about your husband. I am the king. I got this, I got you! I got us!' DID YOU ARRANGE FOR MY HUSBAND TO DIE? How could he have gotten separated from his team in the middle of war? That doesn't even sound right!"

David said, "I assure you that I had nothing to do with this. Uriah was a casualty of war and while his loss is a great loss for us all, this does clear things up for us and the pregnancy. The only people, besides me, that knows that Uriah did not sleep with you when he was home is my servants and they have sworn an oath that what happens in the palace stays in the palace."

Bathsheba said, "When he was home? When was he at home and why didn't he come see me?" What on earth have you done?"

David tried his best to convince Bathsheba that he had nothing to do with her Uriah being killed, but she wasn't hearing it. She felt in her spirit that David was lying.

David had a big ceremony honoring Uriah and presented the highest military medal, the Medal of Honor to Bathsheba on behalf of Uriah. There was a 12-gun salute, and Bathsheba was given an honorary flag that the honor guards precisely folded 12 times to symbolize the 12 tribes of Israel. David also made sure that Bathsheba received a monthly check and health benefits. He did not want Bathsheba to have to tirelessly endure the Veteran System and have to continuously file endless paperwork providing the needed evidence only to be denied time and time again.

Days after the ceremony for Uriah, David was strategizing for the war and thought to himself, "Now that Uriah is gone and Bathsheba and the kingdom has mourned his loss and the time of mourning is over, I think that I can now take Bathsheba out of that apartment of mourning and make her my wife. I am sure that it is hard for her because every time someone sees her in public they offer her their condolences and each time that happens it brings her right back to the place of grief and mourning. It brings it all right back up and she starts spiraling again. I believe that she and my baby should be at the palace, out of the public eye and not in some low class rent neighborhood. They need to be with me and they shall be!"

Remember Shechem from Part two of my original series in Genesis 34, chapter 6, titled, "Baby Girl is Stalked, Raped and Kidnapped", doesn't this sound like the same stuff? First David rapes Bathsheba now he wants her to be his wife? That is some sick stuff, just like Shechem!

David once again sent his servant to bring Bathsheba to him but this time there were added orders. David told his servant, "I want you to go and bring Bathsheba to me, but this time what I need you to do is organize the other servants to go to her house while she is here talking with me and pack up all of her belongings and bring them here to the palace."

The servant asked, "Do you want her belongings placed in the Concubine quarters?"

David replied, "Man no! I want her belongings to be placed right there in the room that I set aside for my wife. I never knew when I would get married to the right one, but I know that Bathsheba is the one. I think about her all the time and now that her husband was killed in war, I want her here with me. I don't want her to be alone."

The servant replied, "Well, I see. You are going to make an honest woman out of this one."

David replied, "An honest woman? She has been nothing but honest and pure. I am the one that …well, I don't have to make anything out of her other than to make her my wife."

The servant replied, "Yes sir! I do understand and we are, I mean I am happy to hear this."

David stated, "Please be sure and keep the marriage part between you and I. I want to surprise her, so have some of the other female servants to set up a beautiful arrangement of flowers, red rose flower petals everywhere, crystal lights and flowing white silk. I want the mood set for the proposal. Got it?"

The servant replied, "I am on it and it shall be done according to your orders. No worries King David, we gotcha back! We gotchu!"

So the servant left and went to tell the other servants what needed to be done. Ya know refrigerators never stop running and neither did this servants mouth! YASS, he told all of the other servants the part about marriage. When he did the ladies had something to say, "Marriage! Really? Well it's about time that he does the right thing!"

One of the older female servants said, "My prayers have been answered. I prayed that he would do the right thing regarding Bathsheba. We are not fools. We know what he did to poor Bathsheba and to her man Uriah."

Another servant said, "I know right! Ain't that some hot off the demonic press stuff."

The servants went about their duties and carried out David's orders. When Bathsheba arrived David said, "Bathsheba my beauty. How are you?"

Bathsheba replied, "I am getting along ok. I miss Uriah, but I know that time will make it somewhat better. I really thought that we would grow old together."

David replied, "I understand. Do you remember the first time that we were together and I told you that I needed someone like you in my life?"

Bathsheba replied, "I do remember that."

David said, "Well I have decided that you should no longer live in that low rent neighborhood, but rather that you are deserving of living in the palace."

Bathsheba said, "I will not live like a concubine and have the entire kingdom talking about me. With the check that I receive I will be fine and able to take care of the baby by myself."

David replied, "Walk with me please."

David had received the signal from the servant that the room was all set for his proposal. The servants were peaking around corners and had their ears to the walls. The journalist servant was taking precise notes, she didn't miss a beat.

David walked Bathsheba over to the event hall and it was so pretty and you could smell the roses down the hall. The servants had done an excellent job.

Bathsheba said, "OMG!! It is so beautiful in here and look at the roses and white silk. This is gorgeous. Is there some special event today?"

When she turned around David was on one knee. Bathsheba didn't know what to think at this point. David said, "Bathsheba, I know that when I first brought you into my presence things did not go the way that you wanted them to, but I fell in love with you at first sight and wanted you to be my wife, but you were married. Now, you are widowed and all alone and I want to be with you as your husband and king. I know that you may not love me this way, but I am sure that in time you will learn to love me as I love you. I am now taking you as my wife."

Bathsheba replied, "But I can't! I just lost Uriah. How can I do this? What will the kingdom think of me? I feel like I will be breaking my promise to Uriah."

David answered, "Uriah has been dead for eight months now and it's time for you to have a new happy beginning. I can't, in my right mind, allow you to stay alone and in a constant state of mourning. I know that Uriah would have wanted you to be happy and not alone. There is no better person in this kingdom that can make that happen for you, than me. And to address your earlier concern, you will not be living in the Concubine

Quarters, but rather you will be living with me as my wife. I have had the servants to place all of your things in the room in the palace that I set aside for my wife, you."

Bathsheba was silent and did not know what to say. She looked at David, looked around the room and said, "Seeing as how you have made everything happen and I do not have a choice, I will be your wife. Let me be clear…I will be your wife, not your concubine and I don't ever want to be taken back into that sex room. As a matter of fact since you say you love me so much, I want the sex room gone."

David got up off of his knees, embraced Bathsheba as he placed the ring on her finger. He then looked at his servants and nodded and said,

"Please take three men servants with you and dismantle the secret sex room. I no longer need it, I have the love of my life."

The servant replied, "The secret sex room?"

David said, "Don't stand there and try to act like you don't know what I am talking about. Everyone in the kingdom knows about it and they probably found out about it from you!"

So the servants took all of the equipment out of the secret sex room and set it up in the spare bedroom that Uriah had slept in, in the servant's quarters. The servants called it "The NOT So Secret Sex Room" and rented it out to individuals who wanted those types of parties. There were many high ranking officials that rented the room. The servants took the money and made a few stock investments and purchased some rental properties. Each of them were equally making money off of "The Not So Secret Sex Room" and of course our nosey journalist servant took plenty of notes. My girl was gonna be rich when she finally published. She finally came up with the pen name, "The Secret Holder but used the short version of the pen name TS Holder."

David and Bathsheba were married. It was the most expensive, lavish and tasteful wedding seen in the kingdom. Bathsheba was trying to get used to being the king's wife and David was oh so happy. He finally had his gorgeous Bathsheba and his son would not be a secret bastard child, but a rightful heir to the throne and kingdom. BUT, was GOD please and happy with what David had done?

One of the guests at David and Bathsheba's Royal Wedding Reception was Prophet Nathan who was actually one of David's trusted advisors. Apparently David only trusted Nathan to advise him on things concerning the Lord because I truly don't believe that Nathan would have gone along with David's plan on raping Bathsheba and killing her husband.

Prophet Nathan had been out on a mission for God and while he was God spoke to him and told him to go back to Jerusalem. He went back and was just in time for all of the wedding events. Just like a true prophet and in true prophetic style Prophet

Nathan pulled David to the side to have a word with him. Nathan said, "King David, a word please?"

David excused himself from the festivities and he and Nathan found a private place to talk. Prophet Nathan said, "Well, I see that congratulations are in order."

King David said, "Thank you, but I know that you didn't pull me aside to say congratulations? Your presence dictates and commands that you have more to say."

Prophet Nathan said, "You are on point today. You know King when I was getting ready to come here tonight, God dropped this story in my spirit and told me to tell you about it, especially since this is your kingdom."

King David said, "Really? Go on then, you have my undivided attention."

Prophet Nathan continued, "There were two men. One was rich and had everything and the other was poor and had one thing that he loved and that was his wife."

King David said, "Go on."

Prophet Nathan continued, "One day the rich man had unexpected company and wanted to throw this company a nice party with food galore and all of the extra after party trimmings, if you know what I mean."

King David said, "I gotcha."

Prophet Nathan went on with the story and said, "As a part of the trimmings the rich man sent his servant to get the wife of the poor man and bring her to be one of after party trimmings. This broke the poor man's heart and he died."

King David shouted, "Who is this rich man? If this rich man lives in my kingdom I will have his head for what he did. Who does that?"

Prophet Nathan said, "Isn't that exactly what you have done?"

King David said, "Huh? Whatchu talkin' bout?"

Prophet Nathan said, "You are that rich man! This story is about you!"

King David said, "Me? How could it be about me?"

Prophet Nathan said, "Oh yeah, that man was you! That is how you moved in on Bathsheba and Uriah!"

King David said, "No, uh-uh Nathan, you got it all wrong."

Prophet Nathan said, "Be careful. I am here representing God. You can't say that God got it wrong."

King David replied, "Oh! EEK, my bad!"

Prophet Nathan continued, "God brought me here with a message for you and it is this, 'I made you king over Israel and I showed you how to escape Saul when he was hot on your trail. I gave you a wife and many other woman to have. Not only that but I gave you Israel and Judah and would have given you anything else that you wanted, so I do not understand why you thought that it would be ok for you to commit rape and murder. Why did you do these evil things? First you raped and impregnated Bathsheba and then you killed her beloved Uriah! You would think that, that was enough for your appetite but NAW, you had to go and marry her after having her husband killed at the hands of the Ammonites our arch enemy'"

By this time David was on the floor in his white tuxedo crying and throwing his hands and leg around as if he were a fish being cooked in a cast iron frying pan. Sometimes those prophetic words can light a fire in your spirit in a pleasant way or, in David's case, in a bad way.

Prophet Nathan continued, "God said 'and because you have committed this evil rape and murder, rape and murder will always be something that your family will deal with. You have placed rape and murder in your family's generational bloodline. Years and decades from now, you family will still deal with this and wonder where it came from.' God also said, 'I will cause you to have a multitude of problems with your current wives and side chicks. Oh yes, I will rip them right out of your hands and give them to one of the peasants in the kingdom and have that peasant have sex with your wife right out in the open for all to see and the peasant will say, 'watch me now and I will show you how the king does it to his wife and side chicks.' You raped and murdered in secret, so you thought, but I saw it and I will punish you for your deeds right out in the open for all to see."

King David was hollering at the top of his lungs, "Please no, please no!"

If there had not been bumpin' bass music in the reception everyone would have heard David in there hollering.

King David pushed past the tears and snot and finally said, "Okay, okay, I did it, I did it! I repent. I am sorry!"

Prophet Nathan said, "I bet you are sorry, but too little too late. The baby that Bathsheba is carrying is a boy and he will get sick and die. That is the word of the Lord concerning you and your evil deeds."

Prophet Nathan left the room and David was still in there crying because he knew that what the prophet said was true and more especially that the word of the Lord that Prophet Nathan spoke was surely going to happen. Nathan grabbed a piece of the wedding cake and fixed a plate to go. I am sure that after that powerful Prophetic Word that he gave King David, the Prophet was hungry!

David finally got up and went back to the reception like nothing happened. A few days later Bathsheba had the baby and it was a boy just as Prophet Nathan said and there seemed to be something terribly wrong with the baby boy, just as Prophet Nathan said. The doctors tried every test they had and could come up with nothing that would say why the child was sick.

King David called all of the intercessors in the Kingdom and in kingdoms and towns nearby to send out emails, flyers, social media posts and to make phone calls to get every prayer warrior and intercessor to join in prayer for the baby. David himself went into prayer.

David remembered how he prayed when he was in the cave hiding from Saul (1 Samuel 22) and how God delivered him from Saul, so he prayed even more, just knowing that God would hear him. David laid himself out on the floor in the prone position and at times he was in the fetal position. He was determined not to get up until the doctors said that his son was better.

Chile King David's family was notified of how David was acting so his family came in and tried to get him off the floor. His mama said, "Son get up offa that floor. I raised you to be a king, not a mop (Man of Problems). Do you know what you look like? Not like a king. Not like the son that I raised. Get up!"

David's brother said, "Dude listen to mama and get up. It's not that serious. Your son is sick but you have the Royal Doctors doing all that they can and you have prayer. Get up. Don't make me get you up!"

Chile look-a-here, David paid them no attention and he then started a fast. He thought to himself, "Some come out by prayer and fasting, so I need to add fasting into this equation."

When his family heard that he wasn't eating they started planning an intervention because they thought that David lost his mind! However before the intervention could take place day seven came around and the baby died. No one wanted to be the one to go in there and tell David what had happened. Not even Bathsheba wanted to be the one! Remember that seven is God's number for completion. So on day seven the Word of God that Prophet Nathan gave to King David at his wedding reception was completed and came to pass.

Special note here: In 1973 U.S. Supreme Court passed Roe v. Wade which gave all pregnant women in the United States of America the ability to choose to keep the baby or not. Here we are in 2022 and the U.S. Supreme Court may overturn Roe

v. Wade. It seems apparent to me that a woman should not be made to keep a baby that is a result of rape. The woman has enough emotional baggage to take care of and who knows if the woman will hurt the baby because the baby reminds her of this evil rape. David raped Bathsheba and the Lord sent Prophet Nathan to tell David that due to his raping Bathsheba and killing Uriah that the baby would die in seven days and the baby died. Who am I or should I say, who are WE to argue with God? Special allowances should be made for women that have been raped and when it is medically necessary to save the woman's life. So many are big on saying God gave us freewill, so then why are we faced with man revoking a woman's God given freewill regarding abortion? I'm just saying and presenting food for thought. Now back to the story.

David started to hear whispering among the servants as they walked the halls to peep their head in and check on him. When the head servant peeped in David asked him, "Hey man, I see you. Hey! Tell me what is going on out there? I hear whispering and commotion. It is really disturbing my praying and laying before the Lord."

The servant said, "King David, I really hate to be the one to give you this news, but your baby boy died early this morning. The entire kingdom is mourning his loss."

David said, "NO!! You say that my baby boy is dead?"

The servant stepped back because he wasn't exactly sure how David would react when he realized what was being said, especially after all of the praying, crying and fasting that David had done. The servant finally said, "Yes sir. It is a sad day for us all. Your baby boy transitioned and went on home to be with the Lord. Your wife Bathsheba is really taking this hard. She just lost Uriah and now the baby. Her grief is even too much for the medical staff to witness so she is all alone."

After David heard that the Lord's word had come to pass just as Prophet Nathan said, David pulled himself together, got off the floor, took a shower, picked out his hair, put some beard shine on his beard, changed clothes and spayed on some smell good, cause smell good always makes things better. After he cleaned himself up he went into the House of Worship and worshipped the Lord for just a little while. After that David could hear his stomach growling, it felt like it was going to touch his back and he began to feel a bit faint because he had just come off of a long fast for his now deceased baby boy so David called in his servant and said, "You know what? I feel very hungry and would like a big blueberry waffle filled and topped with blueberries, two eggs scrambled well, a cinnamon crunch muffin, about four turkey link sausage, a small bowl of fresh fruit and some fresh squeezed orange juice. Could you do that for me?"

Before the servant left to prepare David's food he said, "King David may I ask you a question?"

David said, "Why of course you may."

The servant said, "When your baby boy was sick and the doctors were trying their best to save him, you laid on the floor, cried all night, prayed all night, and wouldn't eat. No one could make you stop or get up off the floor. Now that your baby boy has gone home to be with the Lord you are a totally different person. You have stopped praying and now you want a big breakfast to eat?"

David replied, "I did everything that I could to pull on the heart of God to allow my baby boy to live. I cried out thinking that the Lord would change His mind and have mercy on me and the baby. Now that I know that God did not change His mind and my baby boy is gone, there is no need to fast and pray for him. I can't bring him back to life but best believe when God is ready I will go to the same place that God has taken my baby boy to."

The servant said, "Thank you for answering. That makes complete and perfect sense. I will go and prepare your food for you."

David ate his full breakfast, believe me when I tell you that there wasn't a scrap left on that plate! After breakfast you would think that David would want to take a nap or something but instead he went over to the hospital to see his stolen lover, Bathsheba. He wondered to himself, "I hope that she doesn't hate me for not being there for her while the baby was sick and not being here sooner after he passed."

David reached Bathsheba's room, opened the door very slowly, stuck his head in and went on in to see her. Bathsheba was so happy to see him. Her face lit up with joy and the tears started to flow again for the loss of their baby. Bathsheba said, "It is great to see you here. After not seeing you through this whole ordeal I actually thought that you had abandoned me because I gave you a sick baby boy, but the servants told me how you were praying and fasting for our son to live. I am so sorry that he did not live. Please forgive me!"

And she started crying much harder than before. I guess that she had to go through this alone, but now that David was there she could release all of the pain and hurt of going through the loss of the child.

David sat on the side of the bed and held Bathsheba in his arms and assured her by saying, "I have nothing to forgive you for and I certainly wouldn't leave you. None of this is your fault. It is all my fault. I acted out of lust and I raped you. Yes, it was rape, because it was against your will and even though I told you that I did not have Uriah killed, I am fessin' up and coming clean. I am now telling you that it was me that had your beloved Uriah killed. Please forgive me."

And David started crying as he held Bathsheba. Bathsheba gently pushed David away from her and looked at him while saying, "I knew all along that it was you who killed my Uriah and you are right I did not want to betray my husband, so you acted out of lust and you raped me. I forgave you once I found out that I was pregnant because I did not want all of those negative thoughts to harm my baby. But now you are all that I have. It is you that stands between me and loneliness. Uriah is gone and the baby that I conceived is gone all because of you."

David said, "I promise to always be truthful to you and to always act with integrity in all things. I will do nothing to hurt you any further and will first and foremost consider what God wants before what I want. Thank you my sweet love for forgiving me and my stupid sex-craved ways. I went to the House of Worship before coming here and asked the Lord to take anything that is in me that is not pleasing to Him and make me right and acceptable in His eyes. Gurl look, after all that we have just been through, I am more serious than ever."

Question: Do you think that David will actually keep his promise of considering what God wants above what he wants? This sounds like a sequel!!

It was a few days later that the Royal Doctors allowed Bathsheba to go home to the palace with David. Once Bathsheba was all settled in and feeling better David thought that he and Bathsheba should finally consummate their marriage, get down to grown folks business. David had the servants to make the bedroom romantic and ordered them to hold nothing back in making it romantic.

David went and got Bathsheba and brought her into their marriage bedroom and when she saw how pretty the room was decorated she had the same reaction as she did when he had the room prettied so that he could propose to her. This time Bathsheba's reaction was a tiny bit different because just as David said she would, Bathsheba had grown to love David, especially after she saw how long and hard he prayed and fasted for their baby. She knew that David was able to carry her in the spirit and war for her in the spirit if need be. Bathsheba grabbed David's head and she kissed him as if he were Uriah.

David said, "My, my things have changed for the better. I can do this every day."

Bathsheba said, "Once I saw how hard you prayed and fasted for our son, I knew that you truly loved me and our son. I decided at that point that I needed someone like you in my life. I need you to be the exclamation point in my life."

With that David and Bathsheba got down to grown folks business and Bathsheba became pregnant again with another boy and named him Solomon. Solomon grew up and went on to become the wisest and richest man ever. He is known best, in today's world, for having 700 wives and 300 concubines (side chicks)! How in the world did he make himself available to all of those women? My God it is only 365 days in a year! Maybe I will write a short story about him, I hear he led quite the life.

Even though David and Bathsheba had already named the baby boy God told Prophet Nathan to go see King David and deliver another Word to him. Prophet Nathan went to the palace to see King David and as soon as King David heard Prophet Nathan's voice he started shaking and trembling thinking that Prophet Nathan had another hard word for him.

Prophet Nathan entered and King David said, "Oh no! What did I do this time? Please don't tell me that you are coming to speak death to my baby boy! We haven't gotten over the loss of our last baby boy."

Prophet Nathan said, "Naw, David, it ain't even like that. God wanted me to tell you to name your baby boy Jedidiah which means God's beloved."

David said, "Whew! Man don't scare me like that. We will name the baby boy Jedidiah just as God has said."

I bet that you are probably wondering how the war turned out? Well it seems that Joab was able to take ahold of the Ammonites water supply. We all know that if you can control the water and food you got it made and the people will do whatever you want them to do.

At this point Joab sent word to David to come and finish taking the city down or else he would do it and get the credit. Question: do you think that David was a bit fearful of going to war after what he did to Uriah? Do you think that he was afraid that the same thing that he did to Uriah would happen to him or did he think that God had punished him enough already by taking his son?

So David hurried on over there to Rabbah with more warriors and took the Ammonites and their capital city Rabbah down. Chile the way the Jerusalem News told the story David waltzed right up in there, pulled up on the king of the Ammonites and took the crown right off of his head! The reporter further said that the Ammonite crown was very heavy due to it being solid gold and also that the weight from the many precious stones that it had in it like Amethyst, Rubies, Topaz, Chrysolite and others contributed to the weight.

The story continues and says that after David had the crown he and his men went through the city taking everything of value that they saw. David and his men completely emptied the city of anything that was valuable including the people. This was so important that Jerusalem News went live at five showing how David and his men took all the people from the city and made them Kingdom Slaves. He not only did this to the city of Rabbah, but he took over all of the Ammonite cities and captured the people and took the goods. After the capital city of the Ammonites, Rabbah, was taken it was easy enough to pull up and conquer the other Ammonite cities.

Once David returned home he sat down and reflected and said to himself, "It seems that I am back in the good graces of God. If I were not, we would not have been able to take down all of the Ammonite cities. Thank You God for allowing me back in Your presence and for not taking me out when I acted foolishly. I love you Lord."

Prophet Nathan was not in the area but God allowed him to hear David's heart and God and Prophet Nathan discussed David and what was next concerning David and his blood line.

Point (s) to Ponder: (Heavy Food for Thought) Why did David feel it was necessary to rape Bathsheba and murder her man Uriah? He was the king he could have just taken her in to his Concubine quarters and been done with it, but he went to great lengths to get Bathsheba, but why?

In this story we see that David committed rape and murder, but yet and still the Talmud says that Yeshua (Jesus Christ) came from the bloodline of David…hmm?

Now if you recall, in Part 1 of the series Urban Tales of the Bible we saw that Cain was completely left out of the genealogy of his father Adam because he committed the sin of murder against his brother Abel, what was so different in this case? It would seem that David should have been left out of the genealogy of Jesus Christ and that Yeshua (Jesus Christ) would have come from another bloodline that did not have rape and murder in it.

In Matthew 1:1, Matthew 12:23, Matthew 15:22, Matthew 21:9, Mark 10:48, Matthew 20:30, and Luke 18:38, Jesus is called the Son of David, but how could He be the son of David if David lived somewhere around 1000 years before Yeshua was ever even born? That is some real heavy food for thought. If you get the answers please email me at suprnatrl@gmail.com with Jesus Son of David answer in the subject line!

Why was Joab so quick to take David's orders to take Uriah to the hottest part of the war and leave Uriah? What had Joab done that made him guilty to the point that he felt he had to take a man's life? Yes David was king, but we are talking about unjustly taking a man's life!

Take Away: Do not let the lust of your eyes control your heart, mind and body. We have witnessed what happened to David and his baby son for allowing lusty eyes to rule him. 1 John 2:16 ends with, "…whoever does what God wants is set for eternity." David had to find this out the hard way and I know that I don't want to find my eternal rest in hell. I want to be set for eternity.

Prayer: Father we thank You today for giving us the ability to exercise self-restraint and to not allow our wants and desires to lead us down a path of destruction that will be extremely hard to come back from. We thank You that we have the strength to keep our eyes on You and follow Your lead as we wade through this journey of life and all of its many traffic stops.

www.ingramcontent.com/pod-product-compliance
Lightning Source LLC
Chambersburg PA
CBHW060205050426
42446CB00013B/2999